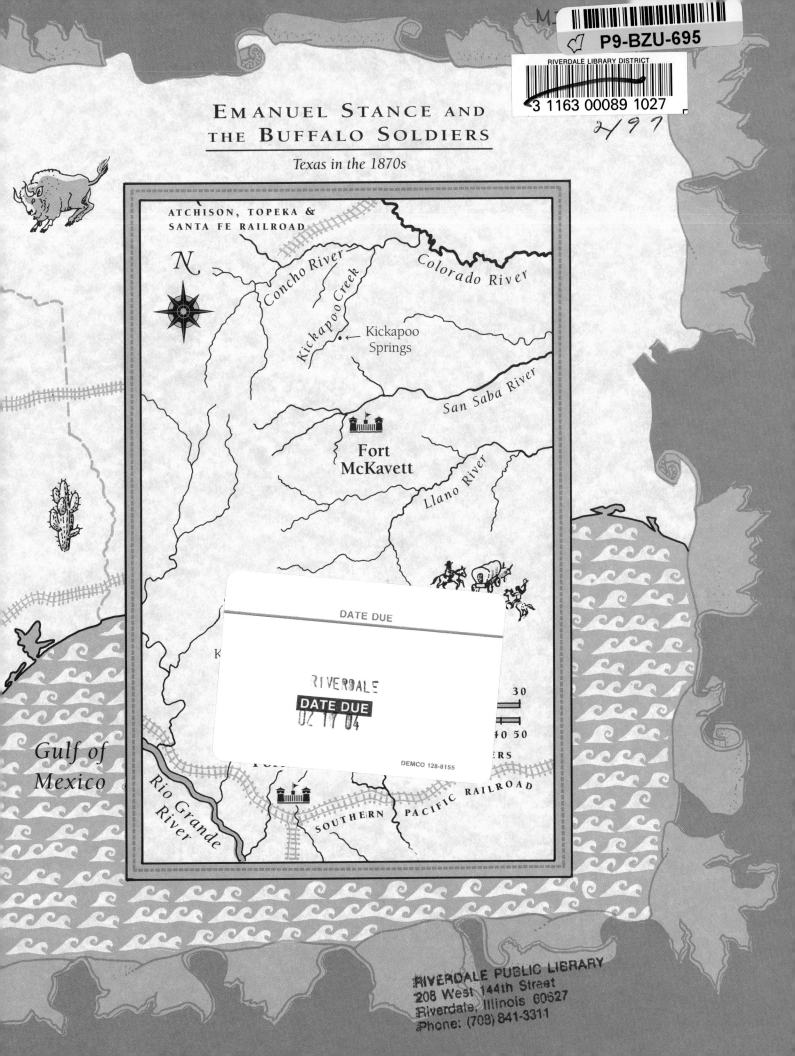

Emanuel Stance and the Buffalo Soldiers

Texas in the 1870s

ATCHISON, TOPEKA &
SANTA FE RAILROAD

N

Concho River

Colorado River

Kickapoo Creek

• Kickapoo
Springs

San Saba River

**Fort
McKavett**

Llano River

Gulf of
Mexico

Rio Grande
River

SOUTHERN PACIFIC RAILROAD

30

40 50

DEMCO 128-8155

Buffalo Soldiers.

The Story of
Emanuel Stance

BY ROBERT MILLER ★ ILLUSTRATED BY MICHAEL BRYANT

Silver Press

*In honor of my deceased father, John Henry Miller,
whose warrior spirit I inherited, and to my
stepfather, Reverend Eugene Boyd, whose patience
I've always admired   RHM*

*A special thanks to Henry B. Crawford of the
University of Texas Tech   MB*

*To Ms. Toni Trent Parker, for suggesting this western series for young
children. Thank you. Robert H. Miller.*

Text copyright © 1995 Robert H. Miller
Illustrations copyright © 1995 Michael Bryant
Map copyright © 1995 Claudia Carlson
All rights reserved, including the right of reproduction in whole or in part
in any form.
Published by Silver Press, Paramount Publishing, 250 James Street,
Morristown, New Jersey 07960
Printed in the United States of America.
10 9 8 7 6 5 4 3 2 1

Library of Congress Cataloging-in-Publication Data
Miller, Robert H. (Robert Henry), 1944–
Buffalo soldiers : the story of Emanuel Stance / by Robert H. Miller ;
illustrated by Michael Bryant.
p.   cm.
ISBN 0-382-24391-9 (LSB)   ISBN 0-382-24400-1 (JHC)
ISBN 0-382-24395-1 (SC)
1. Stance, Emanuel—Juvenile literature.   2. Afro-American soldiers—
West (U.S.)—Biography—Juvenile literature.   3. Soldiers—West (U.S.)—
Biography—Juvenline literature.   4. Indians of North American—Wars—
1866–1895—Juvenile literature.   5. United States, Army—Afro-American
troops—Juvenile literature.   6. West (U.S.)—History—1860–1890—
Juvenile literature.   I. Bryant, Michael.   II. Title.
E185.63.S69M55   1995   973.8′2′092—dc20   [B]   94-28640
CIP   AC

Author's Note

On July 28, 1866, one year and three months after the Civil War ended, the United States Congress voted to add four all-black infantry regiments to the army. They were the Twenty-fourth and Twenty-fifth Infantry Regiments and the Ninth and Tenth Cavalries. Their first assignment sent the soldiers out West to protect white settlers from Indian raids. But these brave and courageous men soon earned the respect of the Indians they defeated. They were called the Buffalo Soldiers, named for the resemblance of their hair to the buffalo's hair.

Many black soldiers earned Medals of Honor during those clashes with the Indians. But the first to win that medal was a nineteen-year-old man named Emanuel Stance.

In the late 1860s, the West began to grow as fast as a young colt. Settlers loaded their covered wagons, formed wagon trains, and headed for the wide open spaces. All they thought about was settling on the new land. It never dawned on them that the land they were claiming belonged to the Commanche, the Kiowa, the Cheyenne, and the Apache Indians.

Soon trouble started brewing like a country stew, the kind you don't serve at the kitchen table.

Reports of Indian raids on settlers reached the United States government. The government decided that something had to be done to protect the settlers. On July 28, 1866, Congress voted to add four all-black infantry regiments to the U.S. army.

After the Civil War, black people had a hard time finding work. When they heard they could join the army and earn thirteen dollars a month plus food and shelter, many signed up. Among those who wanted to be a soldier was a young man named Emanuel Stance.

Nineteen-year-old Emanuel Stance lived in Charleston, South Carolina, with his mother.

"The army is hiring, and I'm gonna be a soldier," Emanuel told his mother as he packed a small bag. He stood barefoot and barely five feet tall in a pair of raggedy pants. His shirt was two sizes too big for him.

Emanuel's mother shook her head. After a moment, she sighed deeply and said, "Well, I suppose we could use the money. Lord knows there ain't much for a young boy to do 'round here. But you be mighty careful, Emanuel, you hear me?"

"Oh, Mama, you're gonna be proud of me. You'll see, I'm gonna be somebody!"

Emanuel finished packing. He smiled at his mother and looked around the shack they lived in. Then he stepped out the door and started his long journey to New Orleans.

When Emanuel arrived in New Orleans, it didn't take him long to find out where to sign up for the army. Soon he, along with hundreds of other black men, was standing in line to make thirteen dollars a month. But Emanuel wasn't thinking about the money.

All he could think about was wearing a blue army uniform and marching tall. Though Emanuel hadn't fought in the Civil War, he could remember black soldiers marching through Charleston. Their backs straight and their heads held higher than an eagle can fly, they marched as if they were one man. There was something about being a soldier that made you *somebody*, Emanuel thought.

Meanwhile, the two commanding officers, Colonel Hatch and Major Morrow, watched the recruits as they signed up. They knew they had to get the men ready for combat.

Training at Fort McKavett under the hot sun was no picnic. From sunup to sundown, Major Morrow drilled the black troops. They marched in ranks. They rode their horses in formation. And they got so good at firing their rifles and their pistols, not a man in any white infantry could challenge them.

As Major Morrow trained his troops, he felt their pride and determination. He was sure that his troop—the Ninth Cavalry—would become one of the finest groups of fighting men in the country.

At last, the troop got its first assignment. They were ordered to patrol the area above Fort Clark, along the Kickapoo River in Texas. There, the Kiowa and Commanche were raiding wagon trains. They were taking horses and setting wagons on fire.

Emanuel Stance was as ready as anyone to ride out in the morning. During his free time, he chopped wood and carried heavy equipment to build up his muscles. Emanuel's buddies were impressed by his efforts. They knew he had that little extra spark of determination that makes a person stand out.

Early the next morning, Major Morrow and a small scouting party from the Ninth Cavalry rode out, looking for Kiowas. About ten miles from Fort McKavett, they spotted a band of twenty Kiowas heading straight for a wagon train of settlers.

"Left flank to the rear! Right flank, follow me!" shouted the major. Instantly, the men split up. Emanuel led the left flank.

The raiding party of Kiowas was gaining on the settlers, but the Ninth was gaining on the Kiowas. The soldiers galloped closer, then fired their rifles.

Feeling the loss of their men, the Kiowa broke ranks and galloped away.

"After them!" shouted Major Morrow.

Emanuel and his men chased after the Kiowas, firing their rifles until it was clear the Indians were really retreating. Providing cover on both sides, the Ninth Cavalry escorted the wagon train safely back to Fort McKavett.

The soldiers had passed their first test in battle. They faced a fierce group of Kiowa Indians—and won!

"I think we've got one of the bravest and best-trained groups of men I've ever seen in battle," Major Morrow told Colonel Hatch. "One soldier showed himself to be a natural-born leader."

"Which soldier?" the colonel wanted to know.

"Emanuel Stance," replied the major.

For the next three years, Emanuel Stance fought bravely during many battles with raiding Indians. He rose to the rank of sergeant and was highly respected by his men.

On May 20, 1870, a man named Captain Carroll, Sergeant Emanuel Stance, and a small group of black soldiers went out in search of some government horses. The horses had been taken by a Commanche raiding party. Spotting something in the distance, Captain Carroll brought his men to a halt. Reaching for his field glasses, he looked down the road. "Just as I thought," he said. "Army horses."

He turned to Stance. "When I give the word, we charge," he ordered.

When the Indians got closer, Captain Carroll and his soldiers charged the band of Commanches. The gunfire was so loud, you'd have thought the sky was falling. Captain Carroll and his men ran the Commanches into the mountains.

Sergeant Stance and a few other soldiers rounded up the horses. They prepared to take them back to Fort McKavett. But since night had fallen, Captain Carroll ordered his men to set up camp near Kickapoo Springs.

At dawn, the men headed back to the fort with their horses. Sergeant Stance heard gunfire. A small troop of soldiers who had been left to guard another herd of government horses was under fire from a band of Indians. The soldiers were greatly outnumbered.

Stance could see that the Indians would soon take the horses—and the lives of the soldiers who were guarding them.

Quickly, Stance led his men straight into the middle of the attack.

"Follow me!" shouted Stance as he charged head on into the Commanche gunfire.

The Indians fought bravely, but they were no match for the well-trained soldiers of the Ninth Cavalry. They were chased into the hills, leaving the horses behind.

Captain Carroll did not forget what he saw on the battlefield that day. When he returned to Fort McKavett, he recommended Emanuel Stance for the Congressional Medal of Honor. This medal is awarded to soldiers who risk their lives beyond the call of duty.

On July 24, 1870, Emanuel Stance received his Medal of Honor.

He was the first black soldier to receive the medal. And he was the first of a long line of black men who proved their courage, fighting as a trail was blazed westward.